FACEBOOK

FACEBOOK MARKETING MISTAKES

AVOID THESE MISTAKES IF YOU WANT TO SUCCEED WITH FACEBOOK MARKETING

FACEBOOK MARKETING MISTAKES

14 Newbies' Mistakes that are Holding Your Business Down

Startup Jahswill

Copyright 2020 by Eduzobe Jahswill.

All Rights Reserved

This book is part of the Facebook Business Series brought to you by StartUP Crest, a leading business development company with focus on startups and small businesses.

You can access more of our resources at

startupcrest.com

Take Your Business Online Facebook Group

Contact: info@startupcrest.com

+2348033867541

Table of Contents

Introduction
Facebook Marketing Mistakes

Facebook is one of the highest traffic social media sites in the world. That is, if it is not the highest. It is also the number one social media powerhouse as at the time of producing this guide. With this much clout, is it any wonder that marketers are still clamoring to discover new ways to use this site to generic traffic!

Lots of social media sites continue to pop up every day and gain traction. However, Facebook has continued to dominate the social media market. YouTube, for instance, has grown considerably in recent times. Especially because of the popularity of videos. Facebook remains the number one still.

But marketing on Facebook is not as easy as it seems. To market effectively on Facebook, there are a number of different things you need to be doing. And a lot of people ignore those things or just don't realize how important they are.

The worst still are those who don't know what they shouldn't being doing. They seem to be doing everything right, but fail to see any significant results. The problem? They are making newbies mistakes that if avoided, can blow their sales through the roof!

In this guide, we are going to learn about some of the biggest mistakes people make when marketing on Facebook. You will discover how to avoid these mistakes and how to turn them around into the most effective marketing campaigns you have ever seen.

So let's begin.

FACEBOOK NEWBIE MARKETING MISTAKES

Mistake Number 1

Depending Solely on Free Traffic

It is true that organic traffic on social media is relatively easy to get compared to website traffic. However, since are not as easy as they were years back before Facebook new algorithm. In recent times, it has become more and more difficult for your posts to appear on your followers newsfeed even those who like your page and your account, tend not to see your post as much as they used to. And this is because Facebook is working hard to derive as much benefit as possible from ads.

Therefore, if a business relies solely on free traffic on Facebook, they will not likely not see much progress.

Mistake Number 2

Relying Solely on Paid Ads

On the other side of the coin are those who depend solely on paid advertising. It is true that Facebook has a relatively effective ads setup. Well thoughtout ads can definitely perform well. But many marketers seem to think that ads are the be-all and end-all of Facebook marketing, but that is not true. For one thing, many people are "ad blind". They no longer pay attention to sponsored posts. I'm sure you may have seen some posts you like but on seeing they are sponsored, you question it and just scroll past.
Some and simply turn them off and may not see your ads. If you concentrate solely, or even mostly on paid ads, then you'll be ignoring the huge potential for free traffic, which can also be more profitable as you're not going to spend money getting that traffic.

The bottom line spend is: ads are great, but you should put just as much effort into building your organic traffic.

Mistake Number 3

Forgetting that Facebook is a Social Media Site

Facebook is first and foremost, a social media site. Too many people forget that aspect and it causes them to miss out on a lot of potential traffic. You can't expect to just posts and and posts sales messages to get results. You need to constantly interact with your followers, chat with them, reply to their comments and dms.

Be friendly and courteous.

In addition, it is important that you share content that your audience really like. The type of posts that will motivate them to like your posts comment on your posts and share your posts. This will not only make your posts visible because the Facebook algorithm, but your followers' friends will also see this activity and potentially get more likes to your page.

For instance, if you have liked a page or a post on Facebook, sometimes Facebook will show that activity to your friends. If your friends like that too, they're likely going to click it.

So interacting, sharing content that people want to interact with not just selling is the best way to go when it comes to selling on Facebook.

Mistake Number 4

Posting Less Content and Inconsistently

By posting on Facebook inconsistently and inappropriately you tell your audience, "Dear customer, we are busy doing more important things, therefore, we have no time to be human and keep you updated about us".

How do you avoid this mistake? Plan your posts ahead of time. Use a day (say 2hrs) to select topics and subtopics to post about and create all the content. You can then use a scheduling app such as Crowdfire (or Facebook posts scheduling) to pre-schedule the posts. Even if you don't schedule your post ahead of time, creating them ahead of time will make it easy for you to just post when you need to.

Mistake Number 5

Posting Too Often

Posting too often is a huge problem on Facebook. In fact, so many pages have become overzealous with their post that Facebook had to add new algorithms to combat the problem. Some users have had to complain to Facebook that they were seeing too many posts on their feeds from the same account. To minimize this complaint, Facebook had to show only a small portion of a page posts to his followers.

Of course, like we mentioned earlier, this benefit Facebook in the form of paid ads. However, this wasn't the only reason why Facebook had to limit the reach of pages and post. The truth is, some people were posting too often and too much. If you post too often, people won't see all of your posts. And that will be wasted effort. Also, some will eventually unfollow your page. And that too, will be a lost.

To avoid this mistake I recommend that you post consistently without overwhelming your followers with more content than they can handle. Between one to three posts per day is generally enough for Facebook.

Mistake Number 6

Ignoring Facebook Rules & Regulations

Facebook has a number of rules that you must obey. If you want to market successfully without risking your account being banned, you cannot ignore these rules.

Sadly, most business owners don't read these rules and regulations. Those miss a lot of important ones and break down without knowing.

For example, did you know about these rules regarding page names?

Page names can't include:
- Terms or phrases that may be abusive or violate someone's rights.
- The word "official" if the Page isn't the official Page of a brand, place, organization or public figure. (Note: If Facebook assigns a Page a verified badge the Page should no longer use the word official in the Page name.
- Improper capitalization (example: tHe best CaFE). Page names must use grammatically correct

capitalization and may not include all capital letters, except for acronyms.

- Symbols (example: ®) or unnecessary punctuation.
- Descriptions or slogans (example: The Best Cafe - We serve the best coffee in town).
- Any variation of the word "Facebook."

Many users simply don't know that these rules exist. It is true that Facebook rules and regulations are many and can be overwhelming. If you look at the terms and conditions it is quite long and thick, and it can be time consuming to read through all of that. However, if you are serious about marketing on Facebook, it is important that you become familiar with the rules and regulations and obey them.

Mistake Number 7

Not Being Serious

This is a basic mistake that many business owners make. Many fail to adequately complete the business page info. If you're going to go into this half-heartedly, you might as well not go into it at all. So be sure to fill out your profile completely.

It's true that it may take some time to complete your company name, company website, about section, design a beautiful looking cover photo, profile picture and the rest of the other details. But it is well worth it to ensure the information your followers care about is accessible, when they need it.

This also includes your tabs, those tabs that appear at the top of your Facebook page. Rearrange them. The ones that you know your followers may not find interesting you can either remove them or push them down, down, and bring to the top, those ones that you find more useful.

In the same vein,don't be lazy in responding to comments on your post. When people make comments respond to them. Take the time to respond to each and every comment. This will show your followers that you truly care, and that you are a real human being, not just some automated system that is just posting and posting.

If you take a look at some of the big brands that are doing well on Facebook. You'll notice that they are very passionate about what their users post and they respond consistently to such posts.

Mistake Number 8

Focusing Too Much on Vanity Metrics

Vanity metrics such as likes and comments are great for social proof. However, if you focus solely on getting more likes to your page, or more likes to your posts and ignore the big picture, then you're likely not going to do well on Facebook. There are pages that have millions of likes but the oners to not make any profits or money from them because they are not properly cultivated and managed. Whereas, there are pages with small followership maybe a few hundred or a few thousand followers who are making it huge by taking advantage of what their followers really need.

So, rather than focus on vanity metrics, try to listen to what people are saying about your brand. What content are your followers sharing, what content are they commenting on, what kind of comments are they making, how many people are clicking on your link to your website, or to your WhatsApp group, how many are sending you DMs?

Those are what you should focus on because these are what actually yield results.

Mistake Number 9

Using Only Text Posts

One thing you should always bear in mind about Facebook in fact all social media sites is the increasing priority to visual content. Facebook users don't like long text. They like things to be short and sweet, straight to the point.

So, whenever you want to post on Facebook, if is a text, make sure it is not more than 500 words long. Sometimes you may even use pictures to tell a story that you would have used a long text to describe. Like they say "a picture is worth a thousand words".

So use other media types (photos, videos, infographics, etc) to attract attention and keep text to a minimum. Social media is not the place for long post. Shorts and straight to the point make more impact.

Mistake Number 10

Not Focusing on Brand Image

Too many Facebook users post irrelevant content simply to get attention. But this is a big mistake. Your Facebook business needs to be known for something. Your posts should be strategically focused on promoting your brand image.

You don't want to be posting about Skin care this week, next week leadership, the week after that fairly used clothes!

Its okay to once in awhile post the odd picture, share the controversial post or share a thought on trending issues.

The key however, is to make sure that you can somehow link all of these to your brand. If you are selling a cookbook, for instance, post recipes and pictures of food, or if you are selling beauty care products post pictures of beautiful ladies, beautiful skin and other related things that can contribute to your brand image.

Mistake Number 11

Not Focusing on Facebook Insights

Do you know that on your Facebook page, there are insights, where you can get access to useful data that are invaluable in your marketing?

Facebook offer those insights for a reason. The data they offer can tell you a lot about your followers and what you can do to be able to reach them and connect more.

One very important metric is the engagement metric that tells you when your followers are mostly online on Facebook.

Now, when you know when your followers are mostly on line. You try to post at those times. Many more are therefore able to engage with your posts. And if more of them engage with your posts it's a double win. One, Facebook algorithm will show your posts to more people because it will tell them that this is something that people want to see. Two, those followers who engage and their friends will see more of your subsequent posts.

Avoiding this mistake can dramatically boost your sales on Facebook!

Mistake Number 12

Not Knowing Your Audience

This is the secret ingredient of Facebook advertising. There are billions of people using Facebook and not all of them are interested in you or your products. If you do not know you're the group of people that are more likely to do business with you, how do you then share content that will appeal to them?

Understanding your audience as a business is just as important as knowing what you want them to do. How will they use your product? What pain points do they have that you as a business need to solve?

To avoid this mistake you can take advantage of free tools provided by Facebook to understand your audience better. Facebook 'Audience Insights' is one of such tools. With this tool you can choose n audience and see it's likes, interests and behavior of the Facebook app.

Mistake Number 13

Being Boring

If all you do is posting marketing messages every day, chances are you are going to fail miserably on Facebook. People want to see posts that are interesting and exciting. They want to be entertained, educated and informed.

They want to share that type of content with others too, and sharing as you know means a largeer reach. So think about some of the different types of content that you can share. Maybe news items related to your brand or your industry, videos, pictures, education, tutorials etc.

Mistake Number 14

Ignoring Negative Feedback

Many businesses quickly forget they have a face and just because users cannot directly point fingers at a particular person, they believe that can do what they like and get away with it. Well, be aware that prospective and existing customers are watching and the way you respond to a disgruntled customer will affect their perception of your business.

Some people take the shortcut by simply deleting or ignoring the negative comments. This might seem like the easier way out, but it only does more harm than good. Over time people will see the pattern and pick up on the insincerity of the response.

To avoid this mistake be authentic and sincere. If you actually fail to satisfy the customer, admit your mistake (after all you are a human) make amends and move on. Even if it is not your fault, recognize the customer's feelings and explain why the misunderstanding may have occurred.

Conclusion

In conclusion, Facebook marketing really isn't all that difficult if you know these mistakes and avoid them. It is true this can be tricky, but it doesn't have to be.

Most people know what they should do to market their business on Facebook. However, many don't know what they should not do. Hopefully with this guide you have discovered some of the things you need to avoid - the amateur mistakes that many people make on Facebook.

Why waste the time posting on Facebook if your post end up being ignored or you end up being banned because of mistakenly breaking one of the rules? So, take time to read and understand the rules, be sure you're posting content that is interesting and relevant to your brand, focus on things that matter like traffic, sales, not just vanity metrics.

You can get a tremendous amount of traffic from Facebook, if you really take the time to market properly.

I wish you the best in your Facebook marketing.

About the Author

StartUP Jahswill
Entrepreneur | Public Speaker | Business Coach

Eduzobe Jahswill Udogbo (StartUP Jahswill) is a trained Physicist with a passion for building and growing small businesses.

He is the CEO of StartUP Crest, a company he formed to help young people start and grow small businesses. He is also the CEO of LabHub Medical Laboratories and Diagnostics and the founding Managing Partner/General Manager of Karone Photo World Ltd, both very successful startups.

In 2009 he setup his first registered company, SwiftTech Integrated Solutions Ltd with the aim of providing alternative power supply to residents of the satellite towns around the Nigerian capital territory, Abuja.

Although that venture turned out to be a total failure, Jahswill learned valuable lessons that have helped him to start and grow other businesses with varied degrees of success.

His number one desire is to help as many young people as possible to discover their entrepreneurial skills and use this to start and grow businesses that will provide employment and livelihood.

His mission is simple: help young people transition from frustrated job seekers and disillusioned startups to successful entrepreneurs.

He promotes financial education that helps young people understand the career options available to them as a means of creating wealth as opposed to the old one-way thinking of "Go to School, get a good job and live comfortably ever after"!

Jahswill appreciates that while university/college education might be a necessity in some chosen careers, it is just one of the options and not the surest path to creating wealth. That is why he advocates learning business and financial skills that gives the best and surest path to wealth creation. He spends most of his time developing content for his various educational platforms especially his blog www.startupcrest.com where he provides valuable resources for startups.

He is happily married and blessed with a beautiful daughter.

Other Books by the Author!

*No Bullshit Business Plan: *How to Write a Business Plan Easily and Convincingly*

*Facebook Posts Engagement Secrets: *20 Proven Strategies to Get More Likes, Comments and Shares on Your Facebook Post*

*Facebook for Business Success: *Top Secrets to Help You Run a Successful Business on Facebook*

*Social Media Content to Cash: *Easily Create Content for Social Media (And Make Money from Your Content)*

*Take Your Business Online: *The Step-by-Step Guide to Taking Your Offline Business Online (Even if You Have No Tech Knowledge)*

Click Here to Get a Copy

www.ingramcontent.com/pod-product-compliance
Lightning Source LLC
Chambersburg PA
CBHW070319240526
45467CB00046B/2144